The *Elvis* Collection

CONTENTS

ISBN 0-7935-9382-4

HAL•LEONARD® CORPORATION

7777 W. BLUEMOUND RD. P.O. BOX 13819 MILWAUKEE, WI 53213

Visit Hal Leonard Online at
www.halleonard.com
www.elvis-presley.com

BLUE CHRISTMAS

Words and Music by BILLY HAYES
and JAY JOHNSON

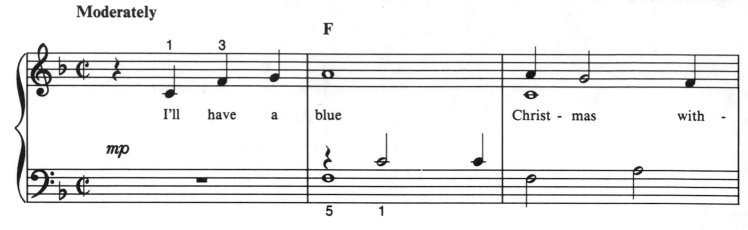

I'll have a blue Christ - mas with -

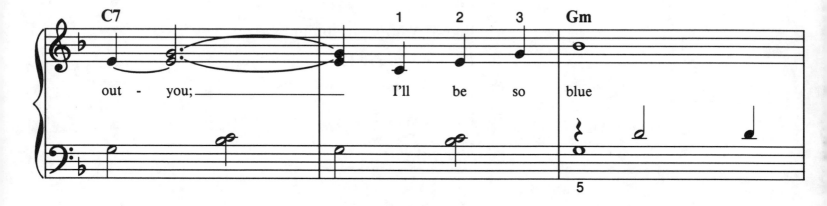

out - you;_____ I'll be so blue

think - ing a - bout you._____ Dec - o -

3

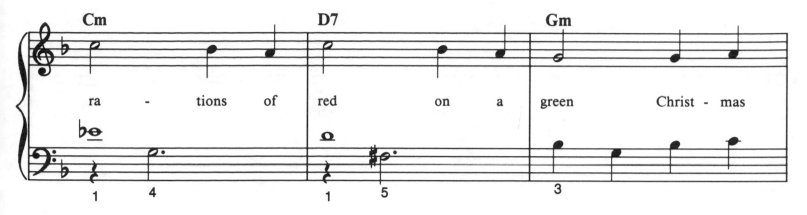

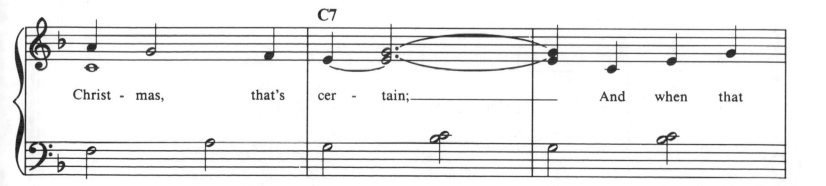

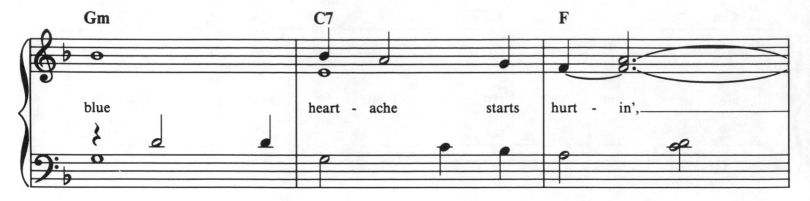

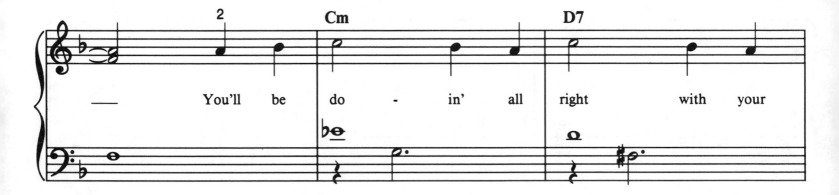

DON'T

Words and Music by JERRY LEIBER
and MIKE STOLLER

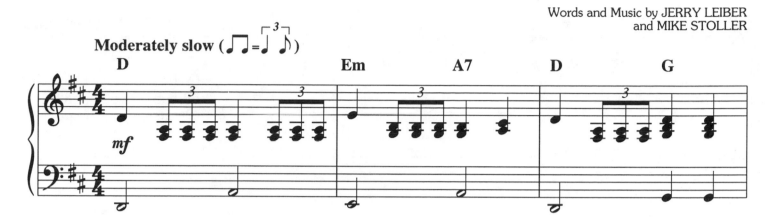

"Don't,
Don't,
Don't,

don't,"
don't
don't,

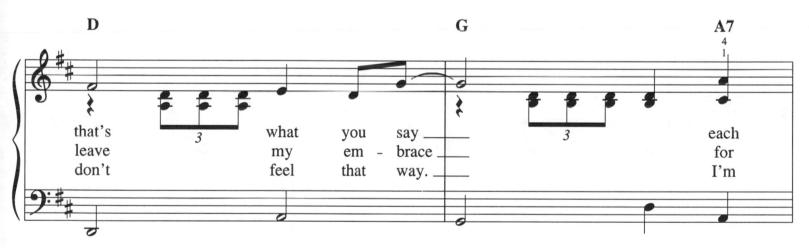

that's   what   you   say
leave   my   em - brace
don't   feel   that   way.

each
for
I'm

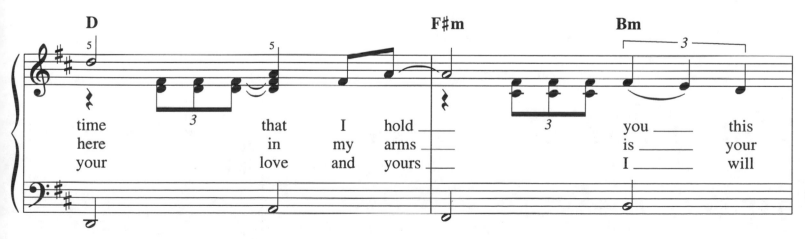

time   that   I   hold
here   in   my   arms
your   love   and   yours

you ____ this
is ____ your
I ____ will

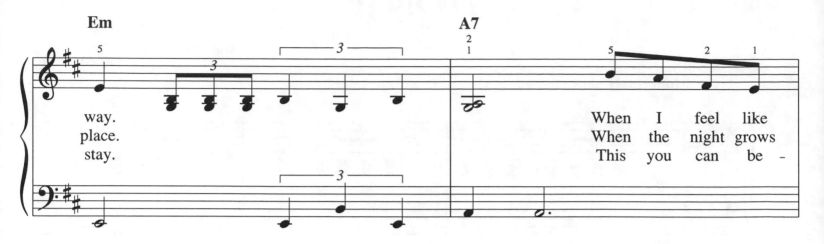

way.
place.
stay.

When I feel like
When the night grows
This you can be -

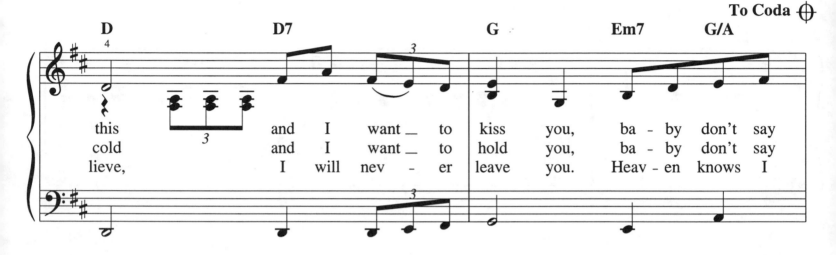

To Coda

this
cold
lieve,

and I want __ to kiss you, ba - by don't say
and I want __ to hold you, ba - by don't say
I will nev - er leave you. Heav - en knows I

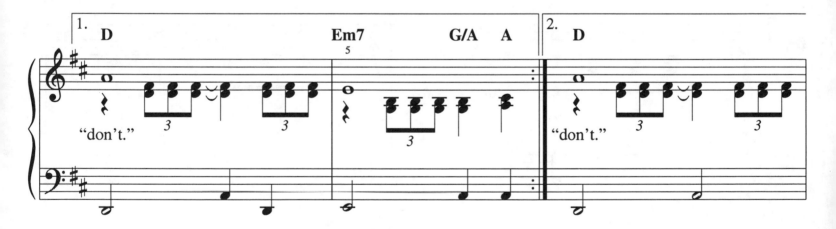

"don't."

"don't."

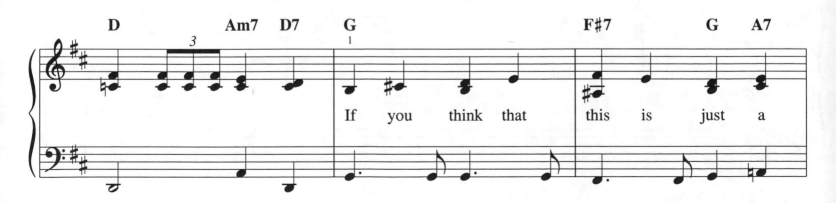

If you think that this is just a

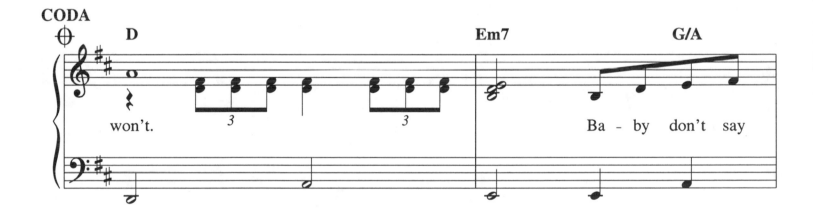

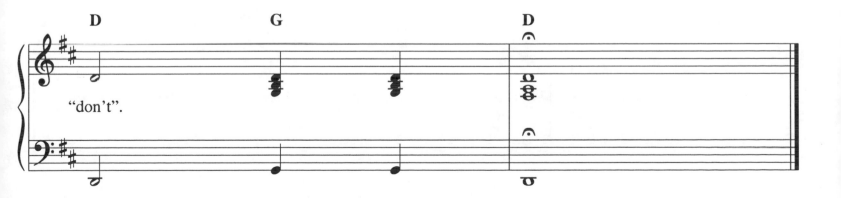

BLUE MOON OF KENTUCKY

Words and Music by
BILL MONROE

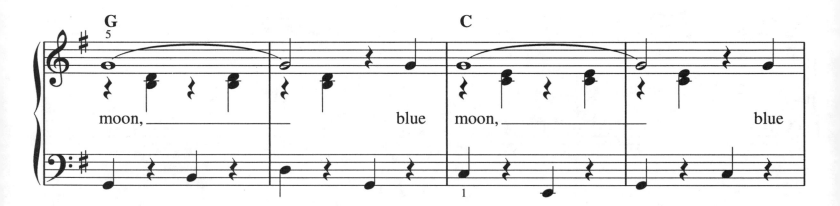

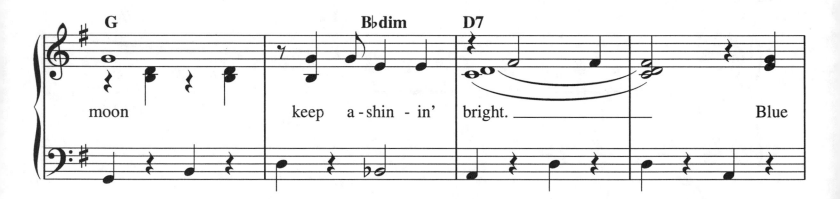

9

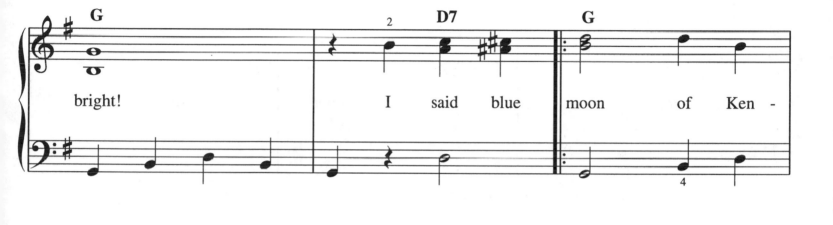

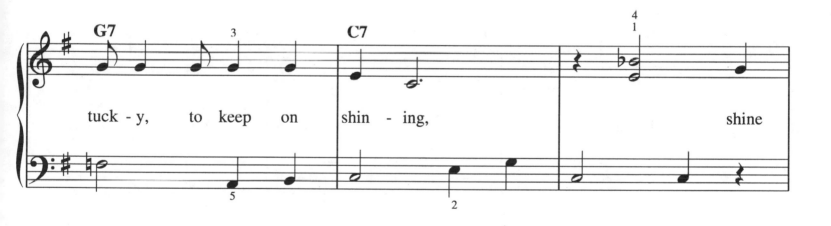

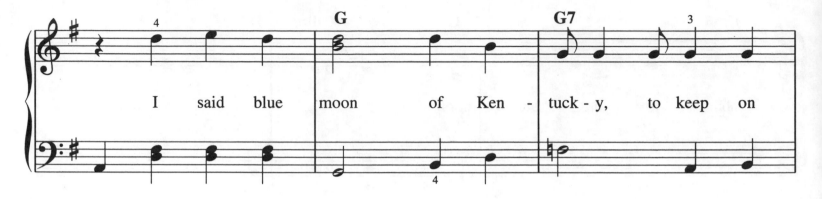

I said blue moon of Ken - tuck - y, to keep on

shin - ing, shine on the one that's

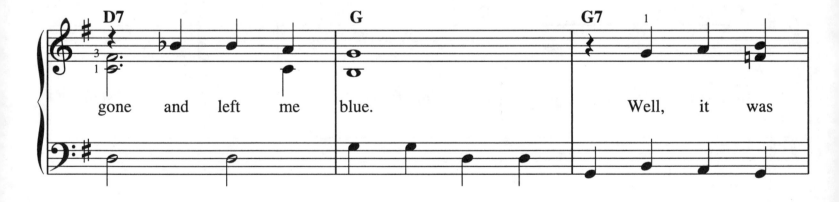

gone and left me blue. Well, it was

on one moon - light night, stars shin - in'

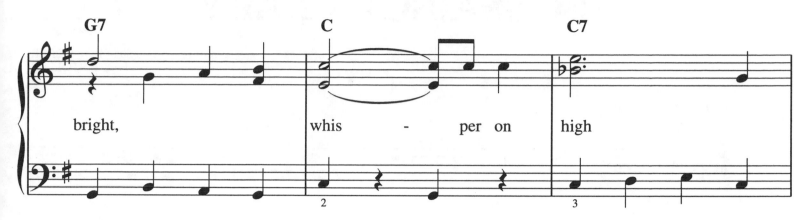

bright,   whis - per on high

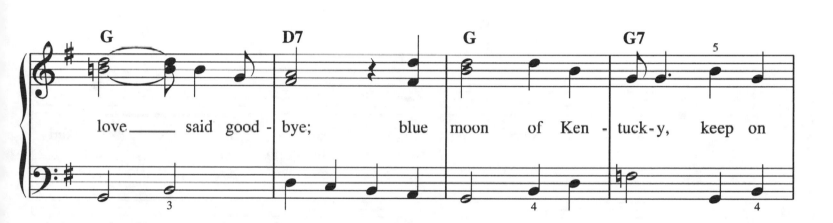

love _____ said good - bye;   blue moon of Ken - tuck-y, keep on

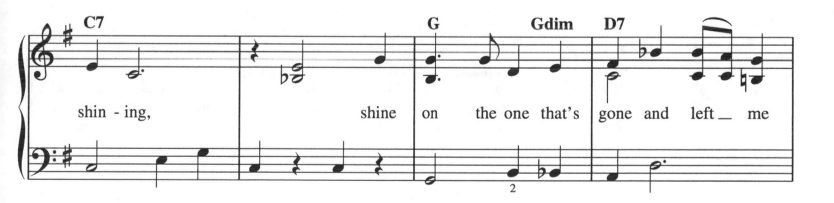

shin - ing,   shine on the one that's gone and left _ me

blue.   I said blue   blue.

BOSSA NOVA BABY

Words and Music by JERRY LEIBER
and MIKE STOLLER

I said, "Take it ea-sy, ba-by, I worked
"Hey, lit-tle ma-ma, let's
"Come on, ba-by, it's hot

___ all day ___ and my feet feel just like lead.
___ sit down, ___ have a drink and dig the band."
___ in here, ___ and it's oh, so cool out-side. ___

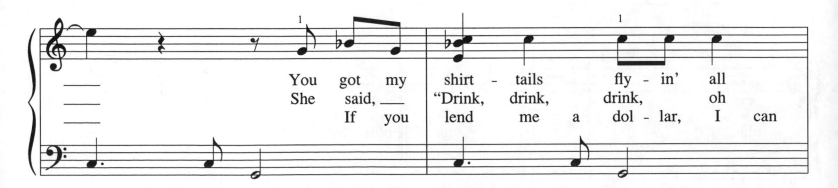

You got my shirt - tails fly - in' all
She said, ___ "Drink, drink, drink, oh
If you lend me a dol - lar, I can

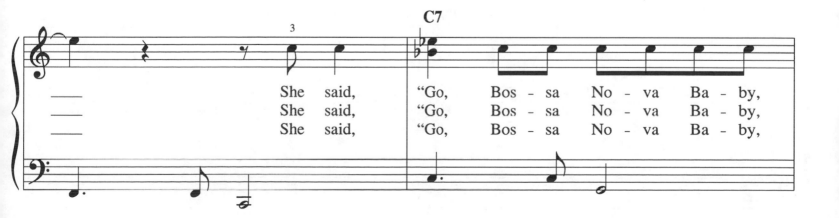

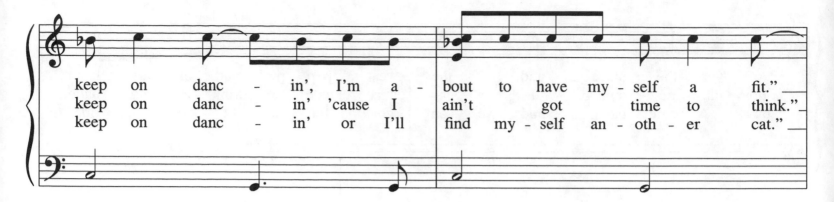

keep on danc – in', I'm a – bout to have my – self a fit."
keep on danc – in' 'cause I ain't got time to think."
keep on danc – in' or I'll find my – self an – oth – er cat."

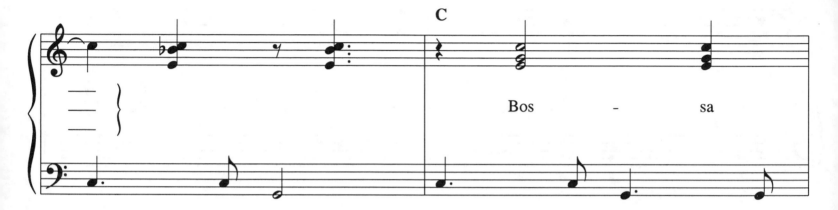

C

Bos – sa

Dm/C   **C**   **Dm/C**   **C**

No – va, ___   Bos – sa   No – va. ___

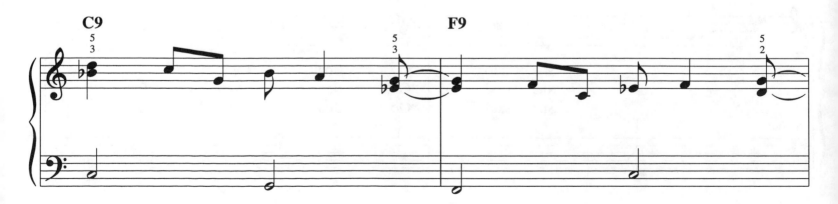

C9   **F9**

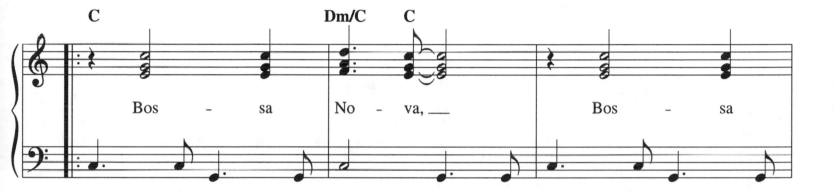

Bos - sa   No - va, ___   Bos - sa

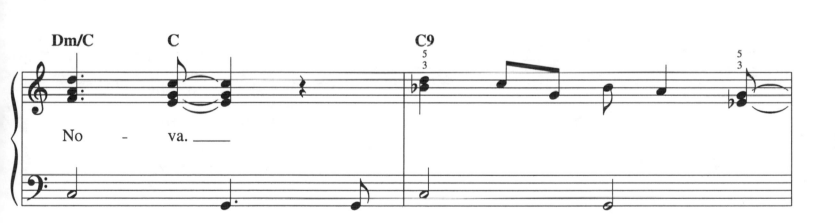

No - va. ___

(Now and Then There's)
A FOOL SUCH AS I

Words and Music by
BILL TRADER

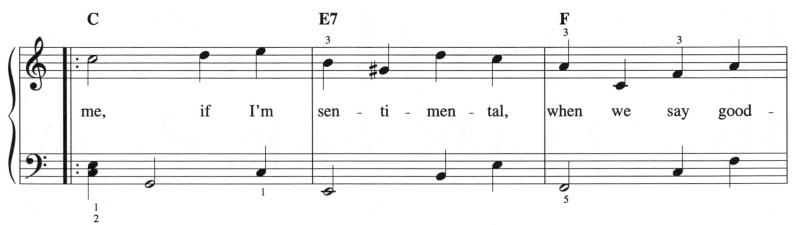

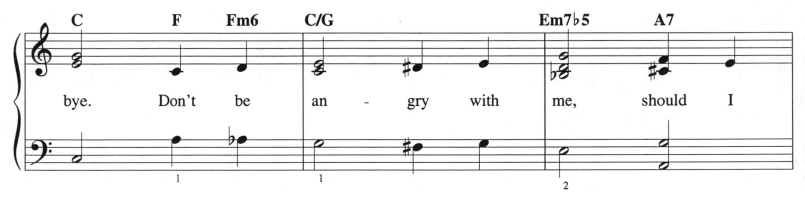

dream a lit - tle dream, as years go by. Now and

then, there's a fool such as I.

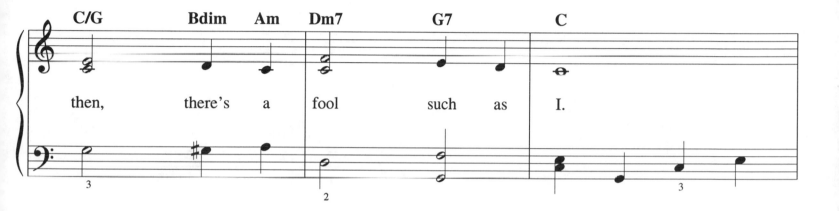

Now and then there's a fool such as

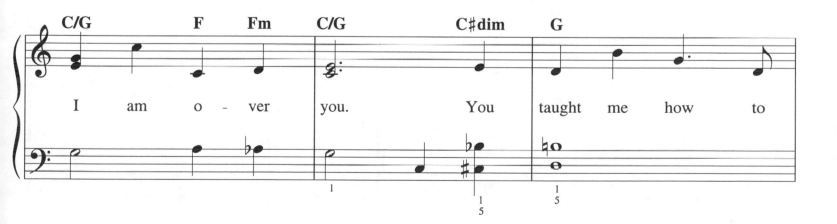

I am o - ver you. You taught me how to

18

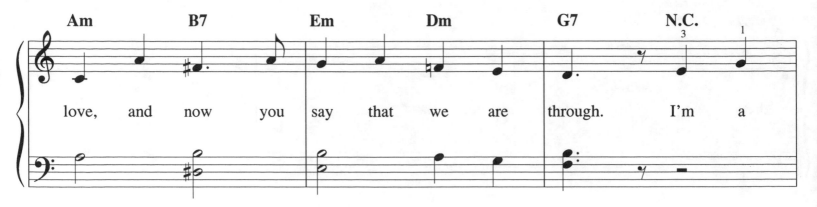

love, and now you say that we are through. I'm a

fool, but I'll love you, dear un - til the day I

die. Now and then, there's a fool such as

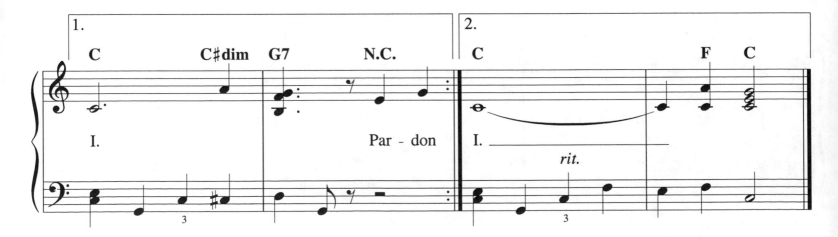

I.   Par - don   I. _____

GREEN GREEN GRASS OF HOME

Words and Music by
CURLY PUTMAN

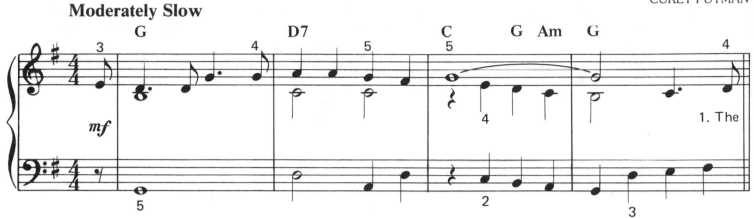

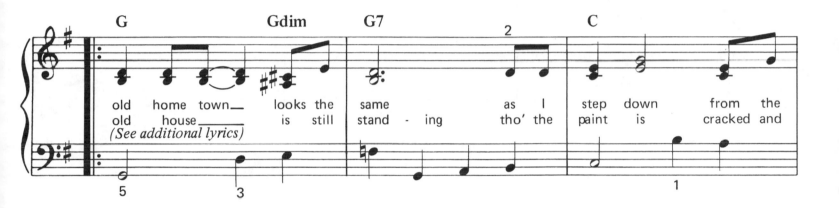

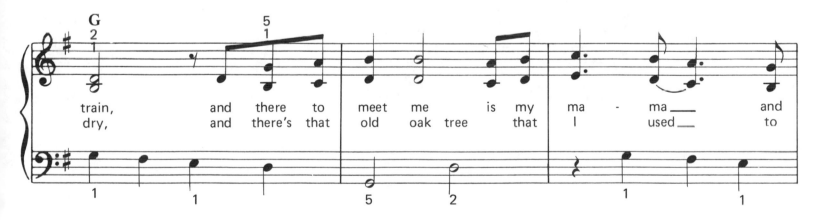

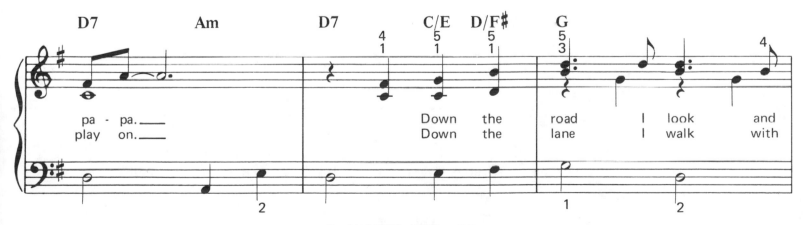

20

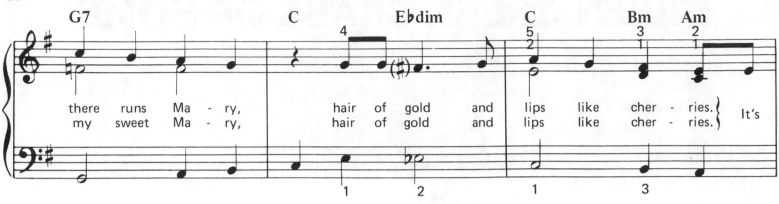

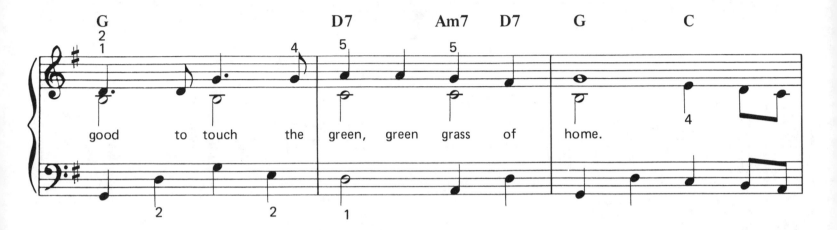

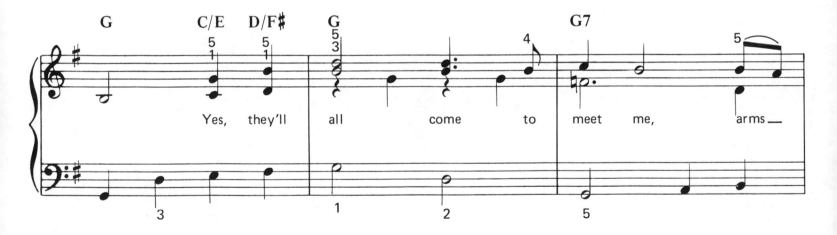

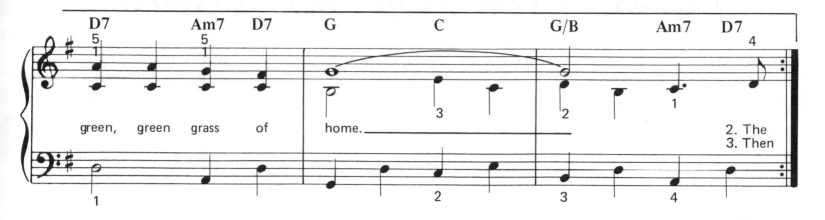

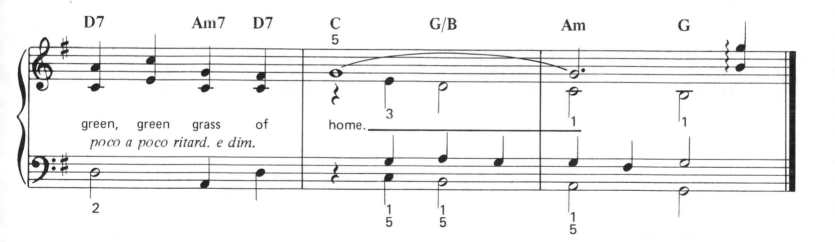

Verse 3.
Then I awake and look around me
At four gray walls that surround me,
And I realize that I was only dreaming.
For there's a guard and there's a sad old padre,
Arm in arm we'll walk at daybreak,
Again I'll touch the green, green grass of home.

Yes, they'll all come to see me
In the shade of that old oak tree
As they lay me 'neath the green, green grass of home.

FUNNY HOW TIME SLIPS AWAY

Words and Music by
WILLIE NELSON

Well, hel - lo there, _____ my it's been a long, long

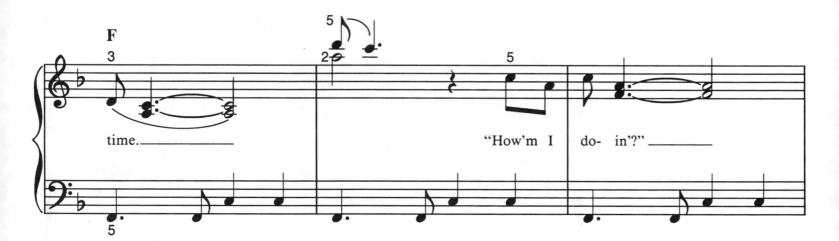

time. _____ "How'm I do- in'?" _____

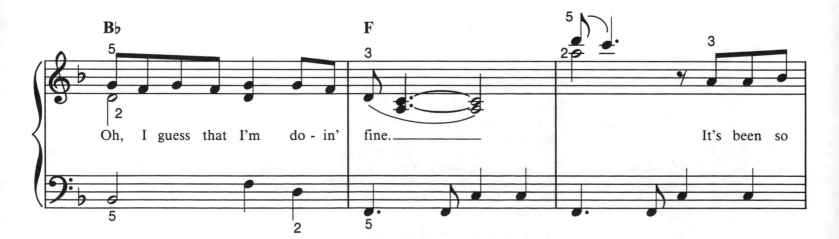

Oh, I guess that I'm do-in' fine. _____ It's been so

long now, _____ yet it seems like it was on - ly yes - ter -

day. Ain't it fun - ny _____ how time slips a -

way. _____

1,2.

3.

2. How's your
3. Got - ta

rit.

Verse 2.
How's your new love, I hope that he's doin' fine.
Heard you told him that you'd love him till the end of time.
Now, that's the same thing that you told me, seems like only yesterday.
Ain't it funny how time slips away.

Verse 3.
Gotta go now, guess I'll see you around.
Don't know when tho', never know when I'll be back in town.
Just remember what I tell you, that in time you're gonna pay,
And it's surprising how time slips away.

THE HAWAIIAN WEDDING SONG
(Ke Kali Nei Au)

English Lyrics by AL HOFFMAN and DICK MANNING
Hawaiian Lyrics and Music by CHARLES E. KING

Slowly, with much warmth

This is the mo - ment I've wait - ed for. I can
E - i - a - a - u ke ka - li nei A -

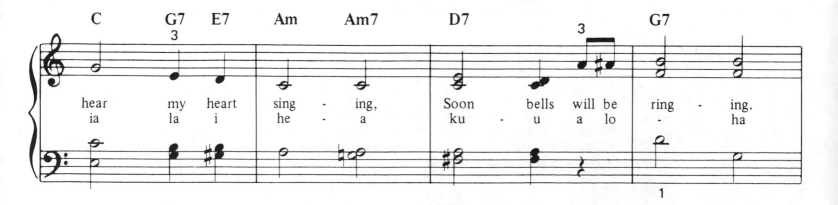

hear my heart sing - ing, Soon bells will be ring - ing.
ia la i he - a ku - u a lo - ha

MCA Music Publishing

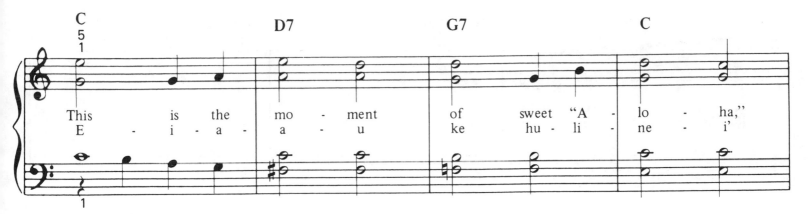

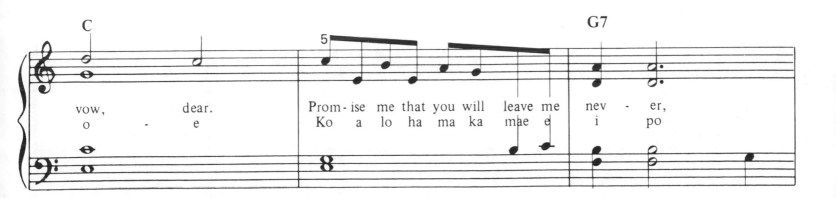

I will love you long-er than for - ev - er.
Ka - iu ia e le - i - a - e ne - i la

Now that we are
Nou no ka i -

one,
in!

Clouds won't hide the
A nou wa - le

sun.
no

Blue
A

skies
o

of Ha -
ko - a -

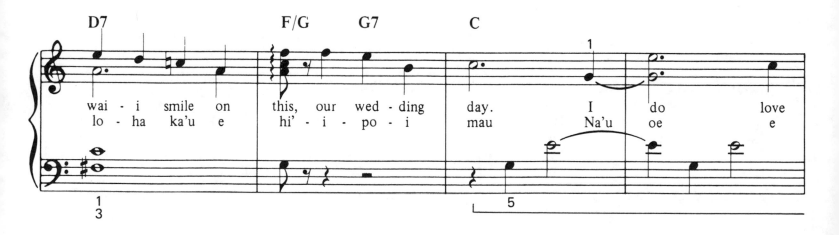

wai - i smile on
lo - ha ka'u e

this, our wed - ding
hi' - i - po - i

day.
mau

I
Na'u

do
oe

love
e

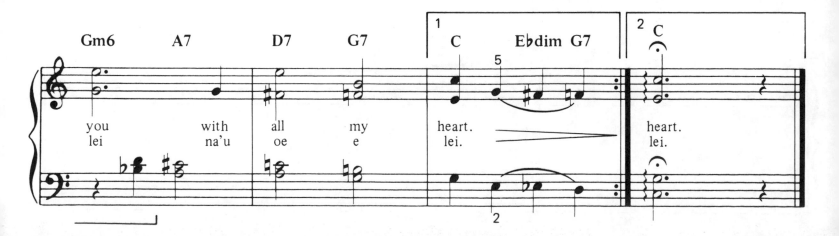

you
lei

with
na'u

all
oe

my
e

heart.
lei.

heart.
lei.

HEARTBREAK HOTEL

Words and Music by MAE BOREN AXTON,
TOMMY DURDEN and ELVIS PRESLEY

Steady blues beat

1. Since my ba-by left me, I found a new place to dwell. Well, it's
if your ba-by leaves ya, and you've got a tale to tell, well, just

down at the end __ of Lone-ly Street at
take a walk __ down Lone-ly Street to

Heart-break Ho-tel where I'll be,
Heart-break Ho-tel where you'll be,

I'll be so lone - ly, ba - by, well, I'm so lone - ly;
you'll be so lone - ly, ba - by, you'll be so lone - ly,

I'll be so lone - ly _____ I could die.
you'll be so lone - ly _____ you could die. 2.,5. Al -

though it's al - ways crowd - ed you still can find some room for
bell - hop's tears are flow - in', the desk clerk's dressed in black. They

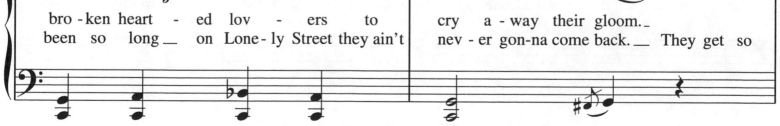

bro - ken heart - ed lov - ers to cry a - way their gloom. _
been so long _ on Lone - ly Street they ain't nev - er gon - na come back. _ They get so

To Coda

They get so lone - ly, ba - by, they get so lone - ly.
they get so lone - ly, ba - by, they get so lone - ly.

They're so lone - ly they could die.   3. Well, the
They're so lone - ly they could

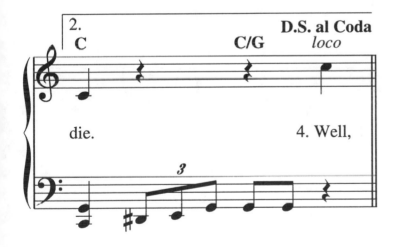

2. D.S. al Coda
die.   4. Well,

CODA

They're so lone - ly they could

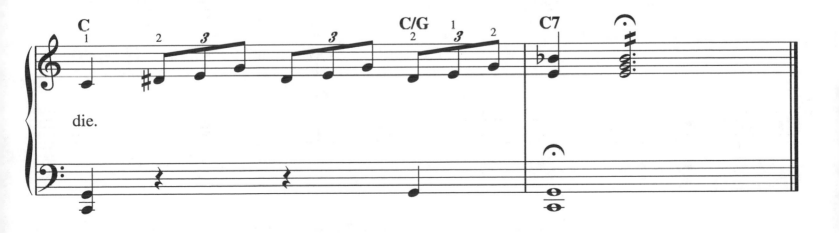

die.

HIS LATEST FLAME

Words and Music by DOC POMUS
and MORT SHUMAN

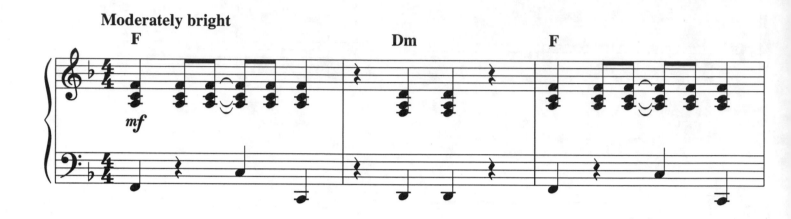

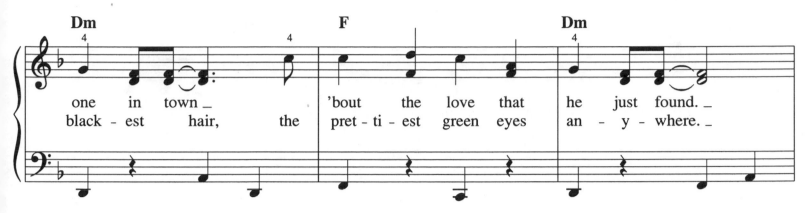

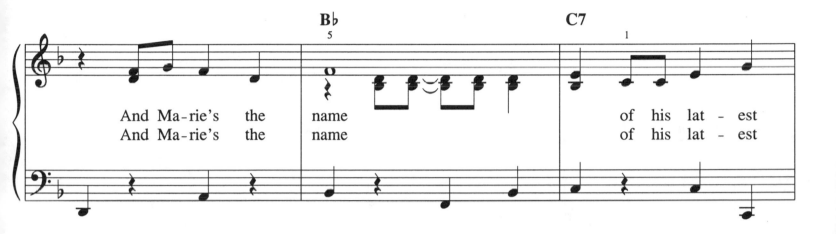

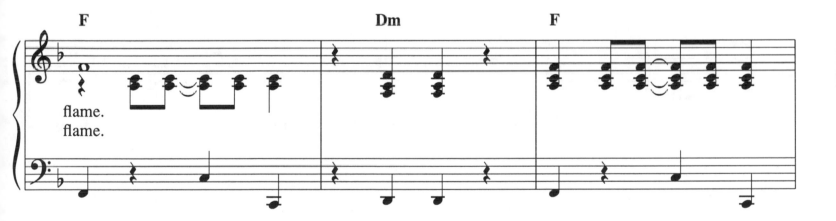

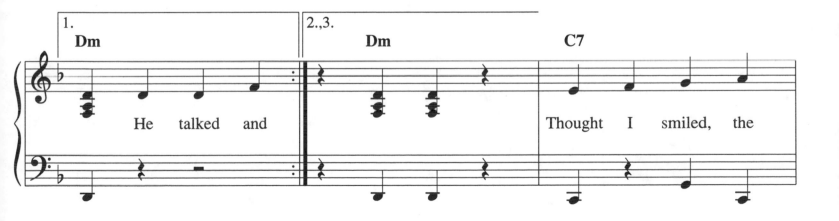

tears in - side ___ were a - burn - in'. _____ I

wished him luck and then he said ___ good - bye. _____

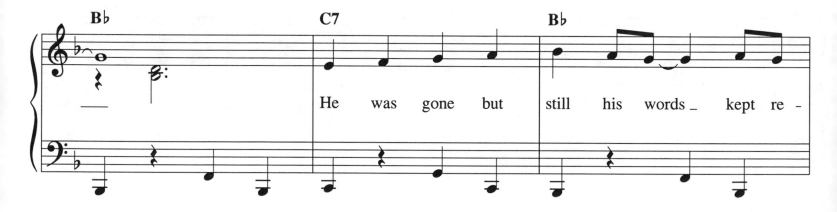

___ He was gone but still his words _ kept re -

turn - in'. _____ What else was there for

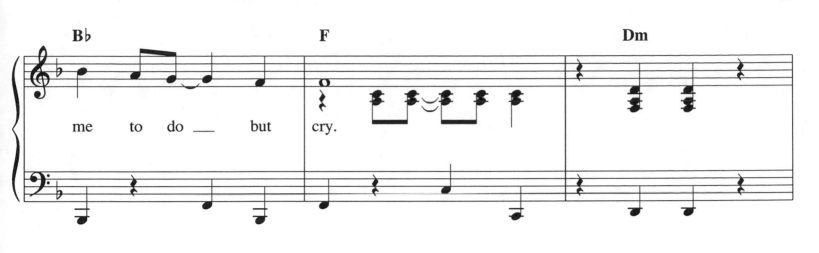

me to do ___ but cry.

Would you be - lieve

that yes - ter - day   this girl was

in my arms and swore to me ___ she'd be mine e -

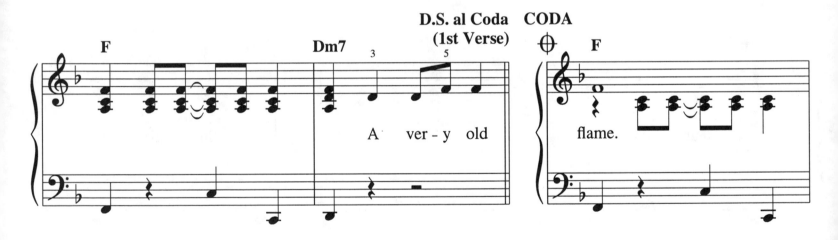

HOUND DOG

Words and Music by JERRY LEIBER
and MIKE STOLLER

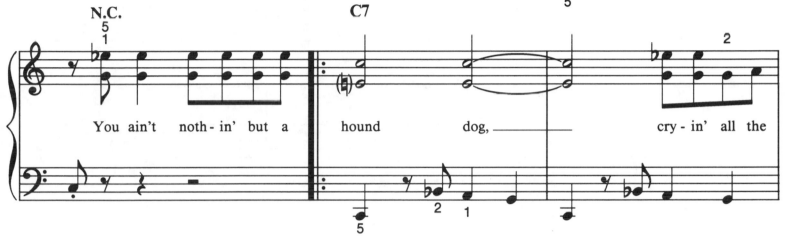

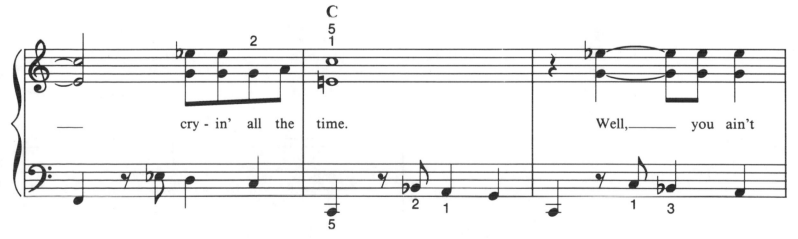

nev - er caught a rab - bit and you ain't no friend___ of

mine. When they said you was high - classed,

well, that was just a lie. When they said you was

high - classed, well, that was just a

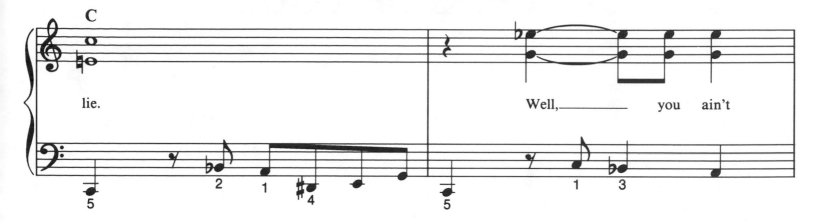

lie.   Well,_____ you ain't

nev - er caught a   rab - bit and you   ain't   no   friend___ of

mine.   You ain't   noth - in' but a

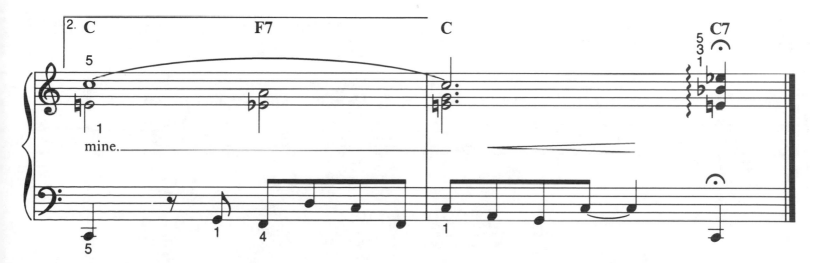

mine._____

I BEG OF YOU

Words and Music by ROSE MARIE McCOY
and KELLY OWENS

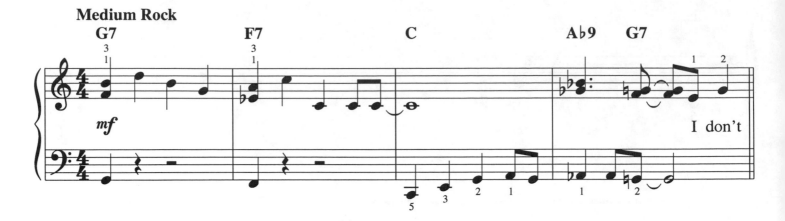

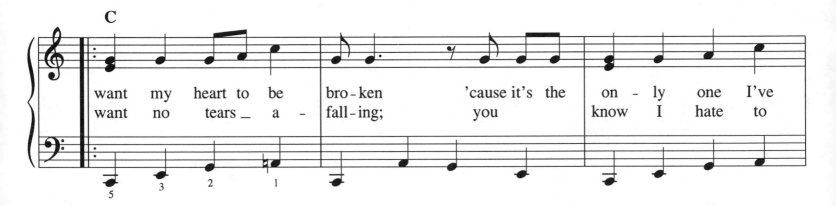

heart, I beg of you.
bye, I beg of you.

I don't

Hold my hand and

prom-ise   that you'll al - ways love me true.

Make me know you   love me   the same way I love

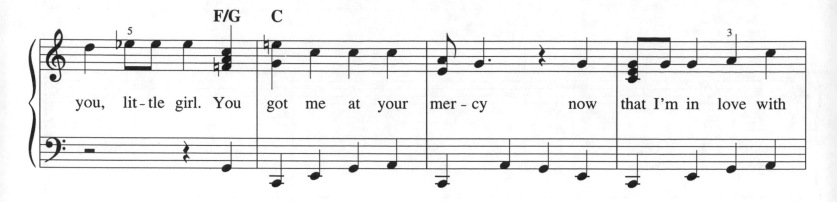

you, lit - tle girl. You   got me at your mer - cy   now   that I'm in love with

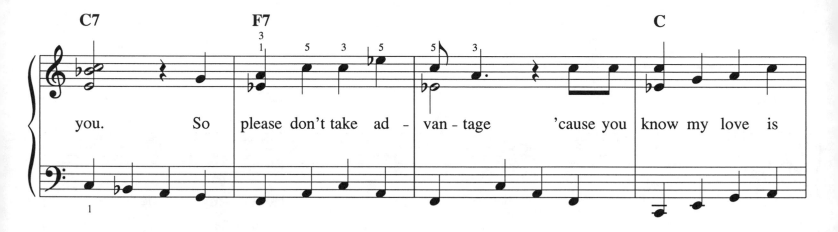

you.   So   please don't take ad – van - tage   'cause you know my love is

true. My dar - ling,   please, please love me   too, I beg of you.

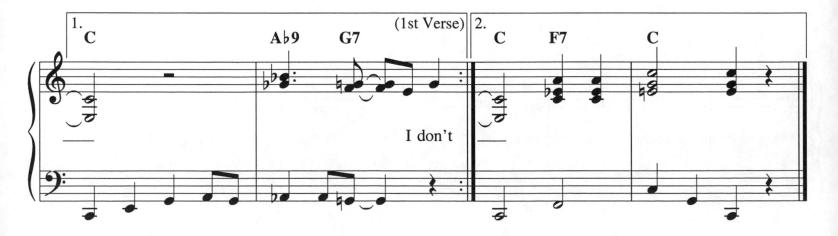

I don't

I NEED YOUR LOVE TONIGHT

Words and Music by SID WAYNE
and BIX REICHNER

Moderately bright rock

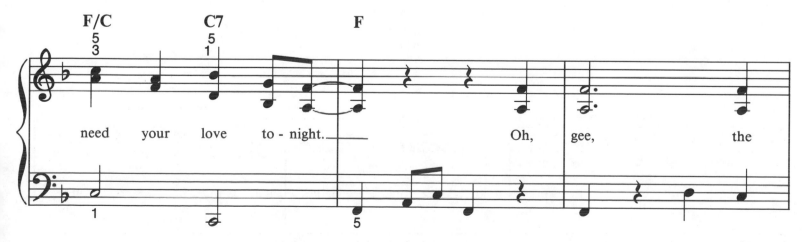

way you kiss.__ Swee - dee, too good to miss.__ Wow -

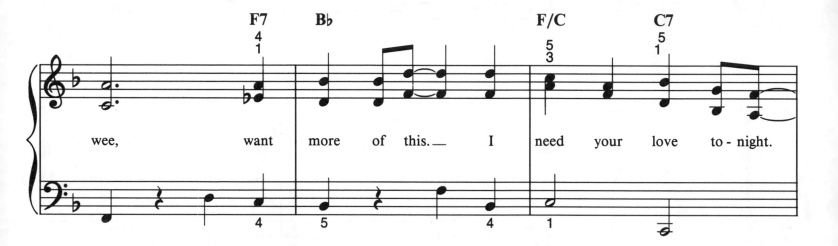

wee, want more of this.__ I need your love to - night.

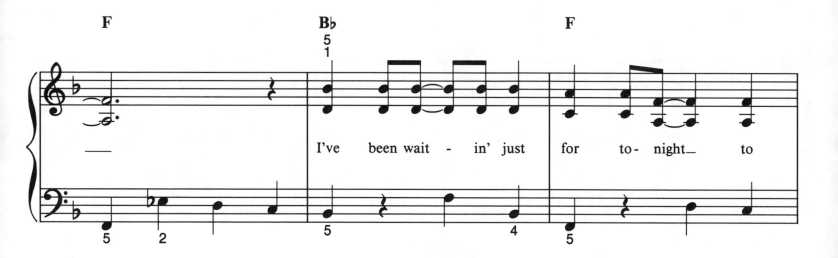

__ I've been wait - in' just for to - night__ to

do some lov - in' and hold you tight.__ Don't tell me, ba - by, you

43

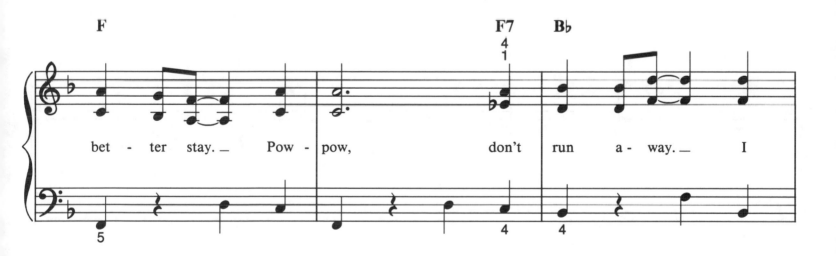

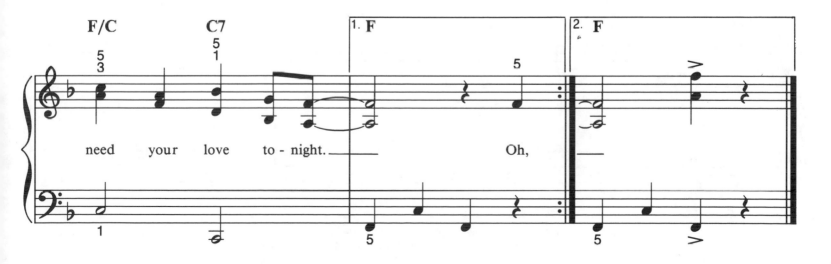

I BELIEVE

Words and Music by ERVIN DRAKE, IRVIN GRAHAM,
JIMMY SHIRL and AL STILLMAN

Moderately, with much expression

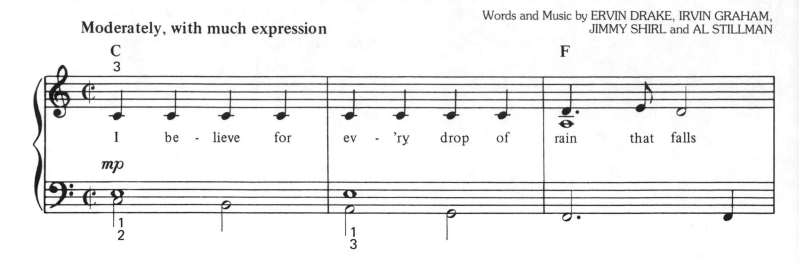

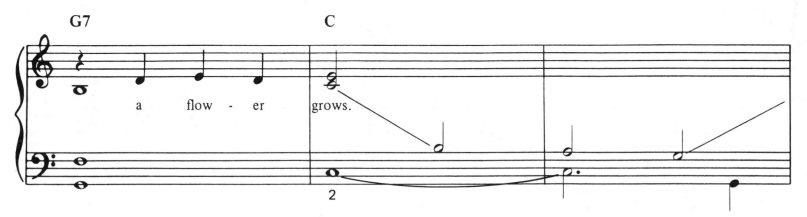

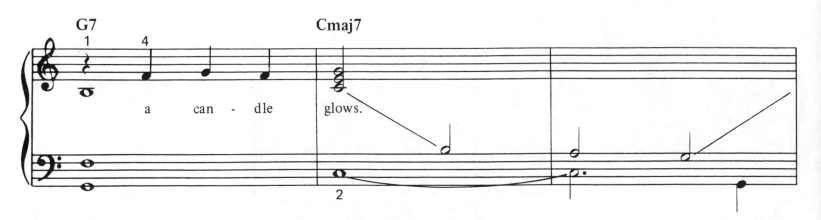

I be - lieve for ev - 'ry one who goes a - stray,

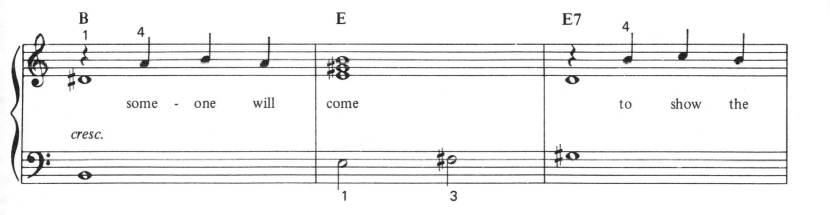

some - one will come to show the

cresc.

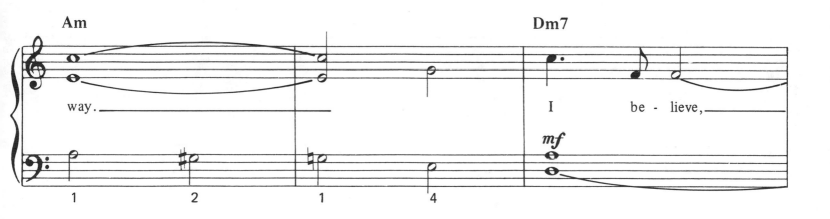

way. I be - lieve,

mf

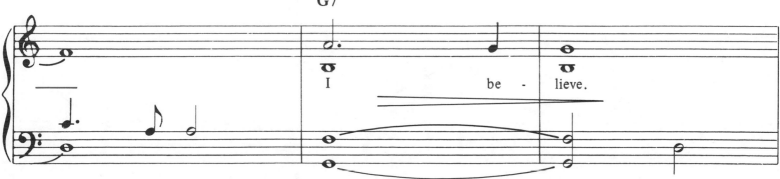

I be - lieve.

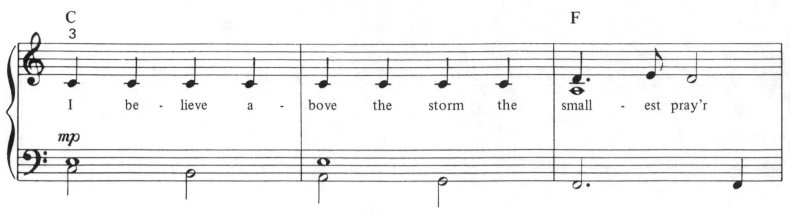

I be-lieve a-bove the storm the small-est pray'r

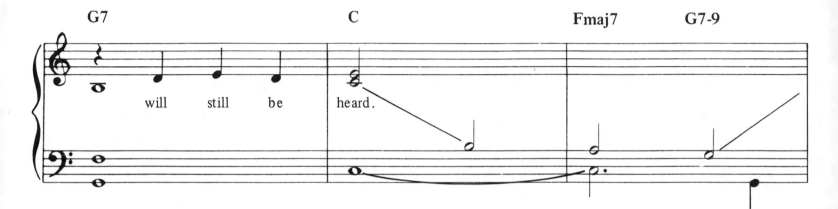

will still be heard.

I be-lieve that some-one in the great some-where

hears ev-'ry word.

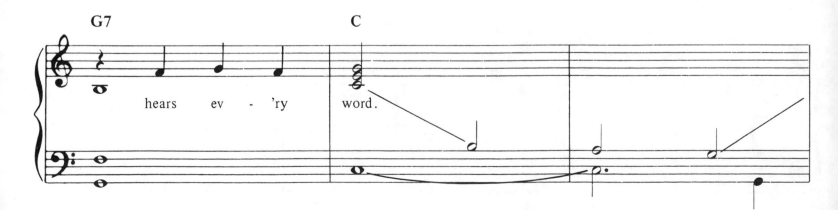

F

Ev - 'ry time I hear a new-born ba - by cry

poco a poco cresc.

B7   **E**   **E7**

or touch a leaf,   or see the

Am7   **Dm7**

sky,_____ then I know why

ff

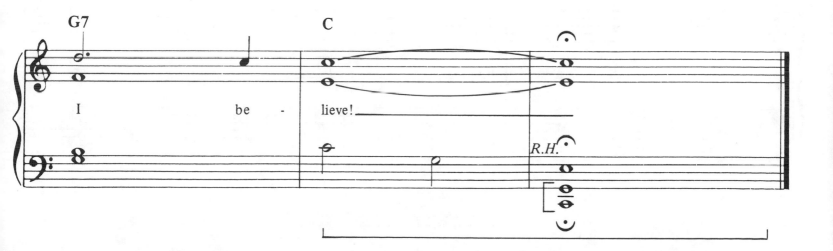

G7   **C**

I be - lieve!_____

R.H.

I'M LEFT, YOU'RE RIGHT, SHE'S GONE

Words and Music by STANLEY A. KESLER
and WILLIAM E. TAYLOR

Moderately bright

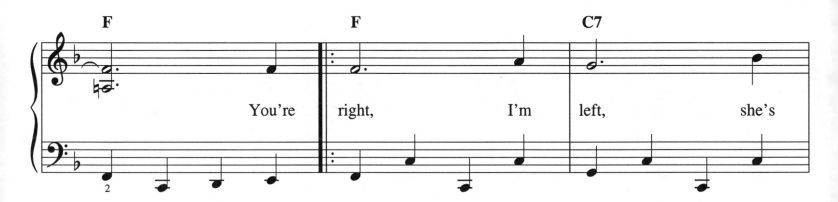

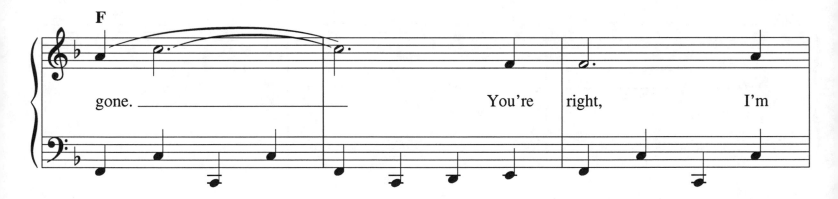

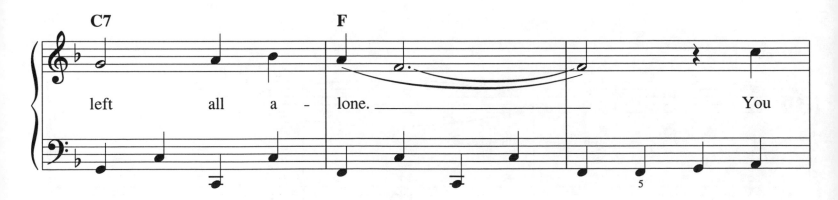

tried to tell me so, but how was I to

know that she _____ was not the one for

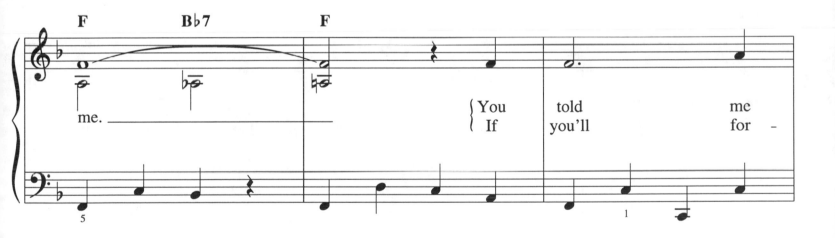

me. _____

You told me
If you'll for -

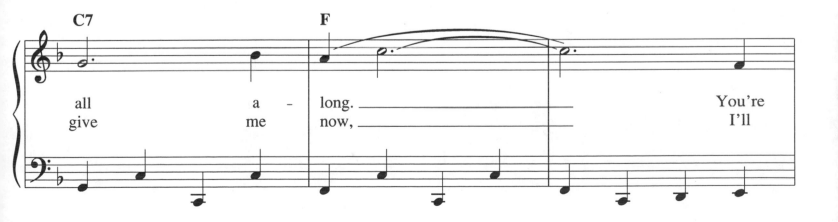

all a - long. _____ You're
give me now, _____ I'll

right,   our love was so wrong. ____
make it up some - how. ____

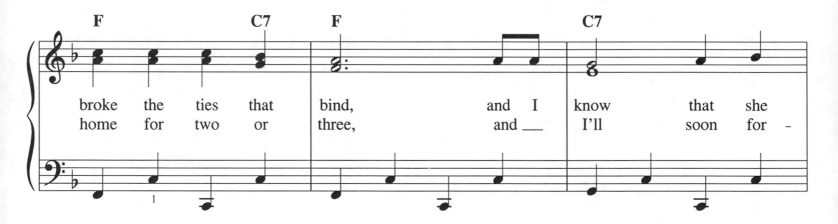

____ But now I've changed my mind   'cause she
____ So hap - py we will be   in a

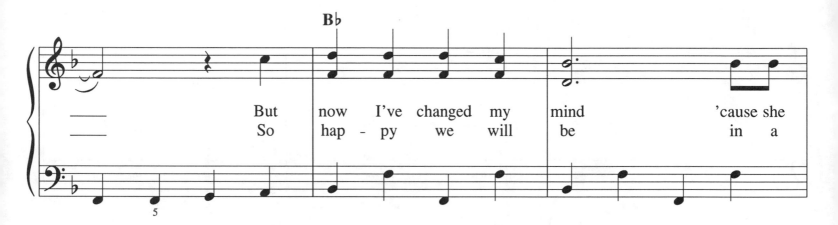

broke the ties that bind,   and I know that she
home for two or three,   and ___ I'll soon for -

nev - er cared for me. ____
get her, now I know. ____   Well, I

thought I knew just what she'd do. I guess I'm not so

smart. You tried to tell me all a - long she'd

on - ly break my heart. You're right, I'm

left, she's gone. _____ You're right, I'm

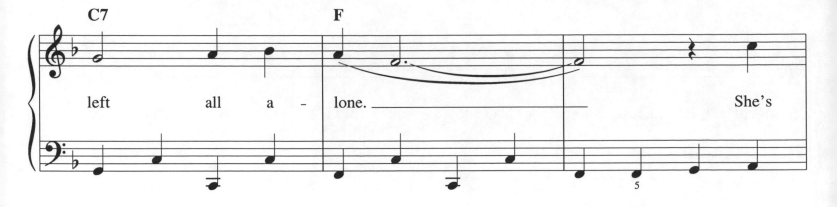

left all a - lone. _____ She's

gone I know not where, but now I just don't

care, for now I have fall - en for

you. _____ You're you.

JAILHOUSE ROCK

Words and Music by JERRY LEIBER
and MIKE STOLLER

54

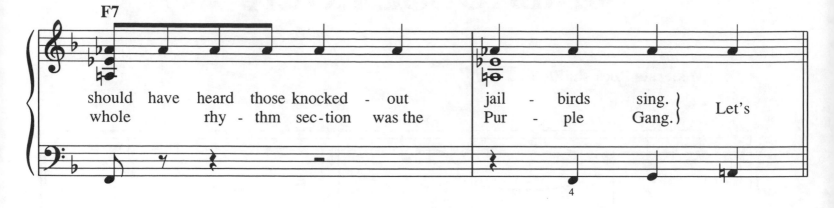

should have heard those knocked - out jail - birds sing.
whole rhy - thm sec -tion was the Pur - ple Gang.

Let's

rock!

Ev - 'ry-bod - y let's rock!

To Coda

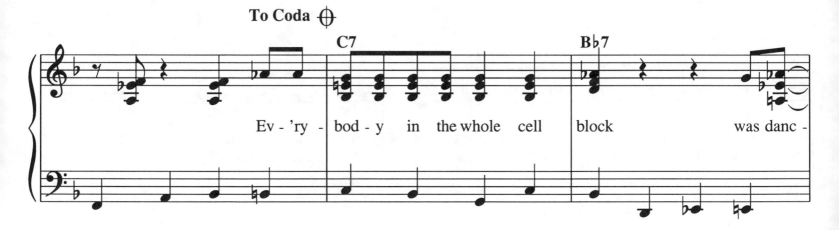

Ev - 'ry - bod - y in the whole cell block was danc -

1.-3.

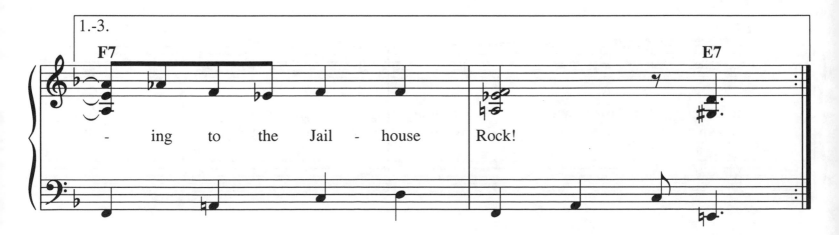

- ing to the Jail - house Rock!

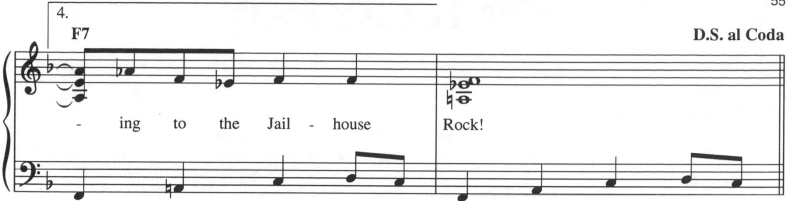

D.S. al Coda

-ing to the Jail - house Rock!

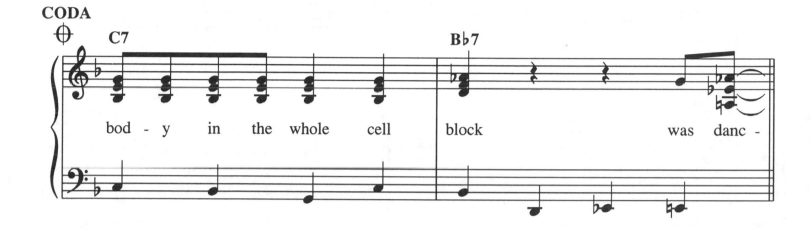

CODA

bod - y in the whole cell block was danc-

Repeat and Fade

-ing to the Jail - house Rock! Danc-

Additional Lyrics

3. Number Forty-seven said to Number Three:
   "You're the cutest jailbird I ever did see.
   I sure would be delighted with your company,
   Come and do the Jailhouse Rock with me."
   (Chorus)

4. The sad sack was a-sittin' on a block of stone,
   Way over in the corner weeping all alone.
   The warden said: "Hey, Buddy, don't you be no square,
   If you can't find a partner, use a wooden chair!"
   (Chorus)

5. Shifty Henry said to Bugs: "For heaven's sake,
   No one's lookin', now's our chance to make a break."
   Bugsy turned to Shifty and he said: "Nix, nix;
   I wanna stick around awhile and get my kicks."
   (Chorus)

KENTUCKY RAIN

Words and Music by EDDIE RABBITT
and DICK HEARD

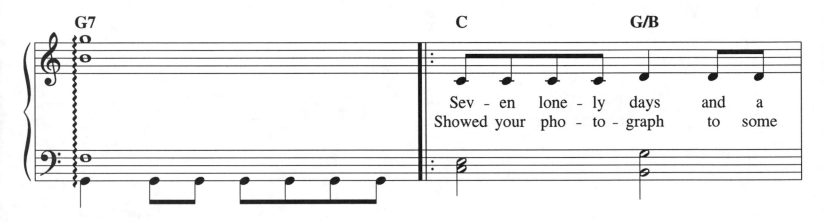

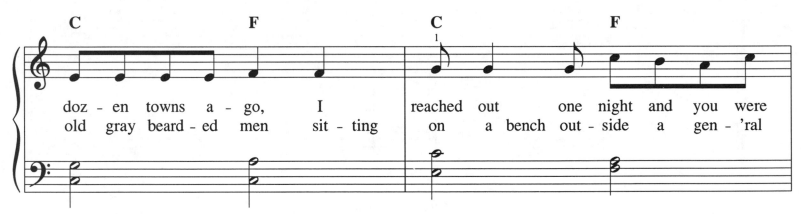

57

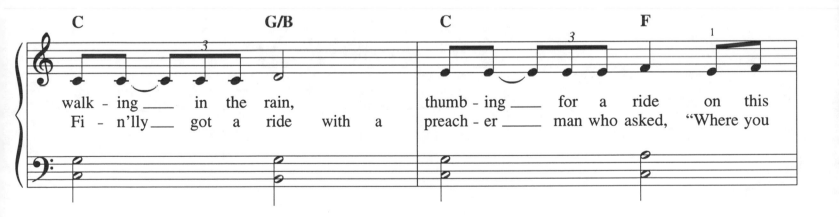

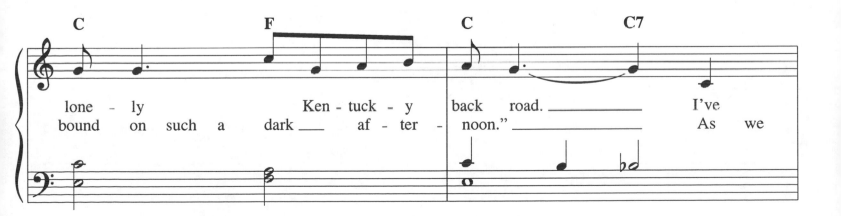

loved you much too long and my love's too strong, to
drove on thru the rain, as he lis-tened, I ex-plained, and he

let you go, nev-er know-ing what went wrong.
left me with a prayer that I'd find you.

Ken-tuck-y rain keeps pour-ing down, _____

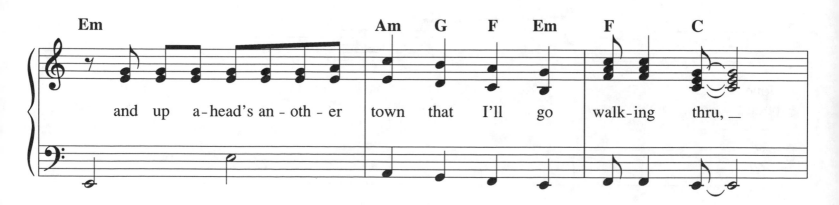

and up a-head's an-oth-er town that I'll go walk-ing thru, __

with the rain in my shoes, search-ing for

you, in the cold Ken-tuck-y rain, _____

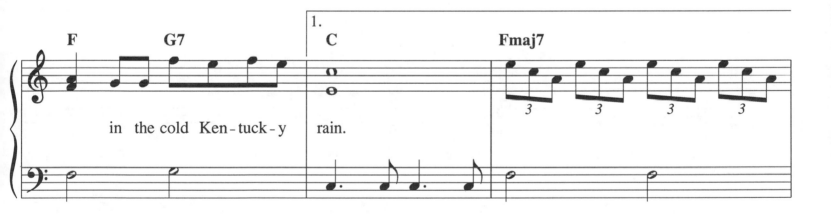

in the cold Ken-tuck-y rain.

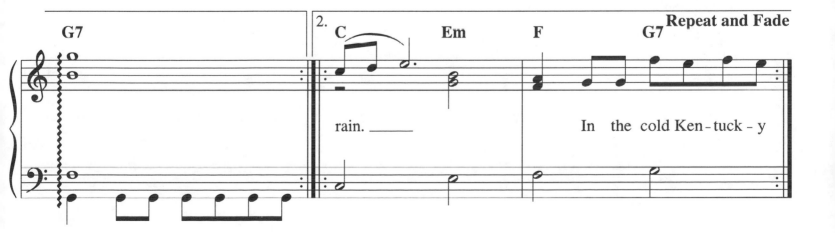

rain. _____ In the cold Ken-tuck-y

LITTLE SISTER

Words and Music by DOC POMUS
and MORT SHUMAN

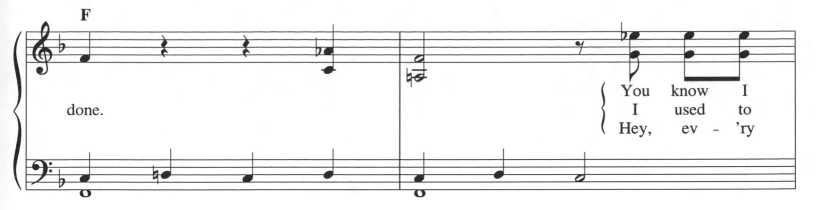

F

done.
You know I
I used to
Hey, ev - 'ry

F7

dat - ed your big sis - ter. Oh, I
pull down on your pig - tails. Hey, girl, ___
time I see your sis - ter, Lord, she's

took her to the show. ___ Hey, I
pinch your turned - up nose. ___ Aw, but
with some - bod - y new. ___ Aw, she's

went for some can - dy, ___ a long came Jim Dan - dy and they
ba - by, you've been grow - in' ___ and late - ly it's been show - in' from your
mean and she's e - vil like a lit - tle old boll wee - vil, think I'll

slipped   right   down   out ____   the   door.
head   right   down   to ____   your   toes.
try   my   luck ____ with   you.

F

Lit - tle sis - ter, don't you,   lit - tle sis - ter, don't you,

lit - tle sis - ter, don't you   kiss me once or twice,

B♭

B♭7   **F**

tell me that it's nice and then you   run. _____   Yeah,

63

LOVE ME

Words and Music by JERRY LEIBER
and MIKE STOLLER

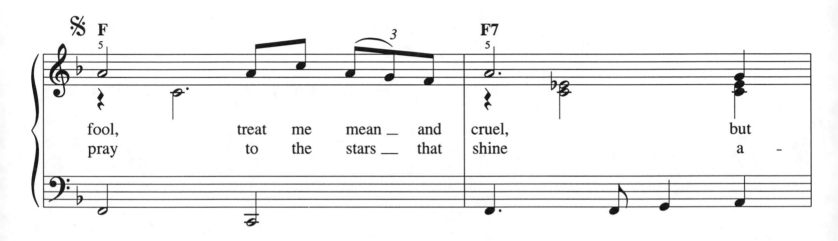

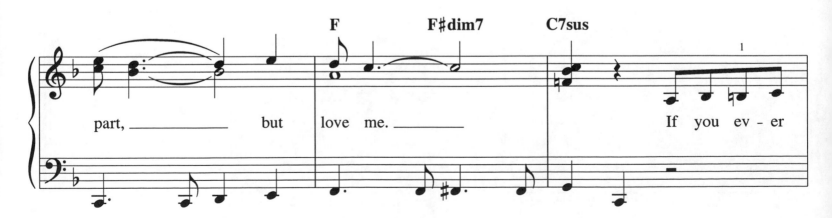

65

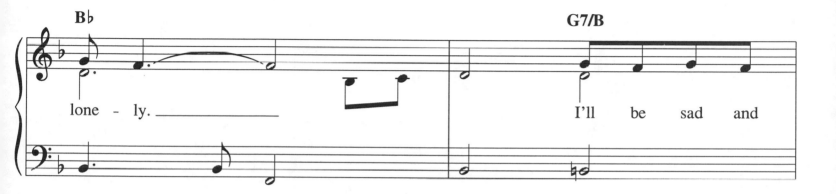

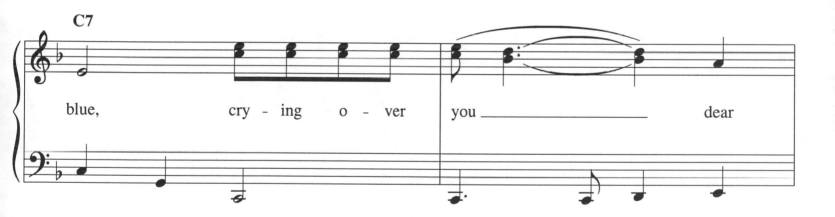

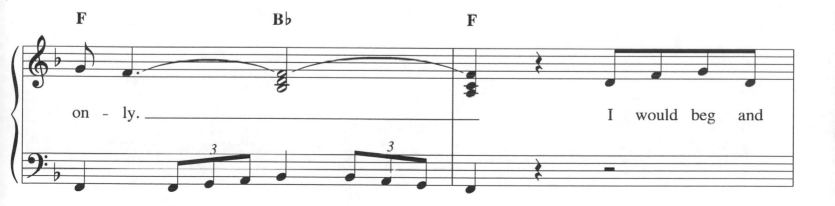

steal

just _____ to feel

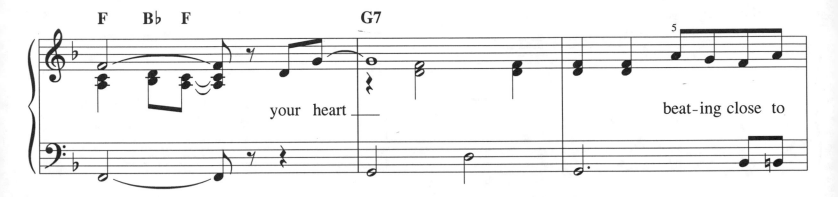

your heart _____

beat-ing close to

mine.

Ev - ery night I

please, _____ please love me. _____

MEMORIES

Words and Music by BILLY STRANGE
and SCOTT DAVIS

Slowly, with expression

Mem - o - ries, pressed be - tween the pag - es of my mind.

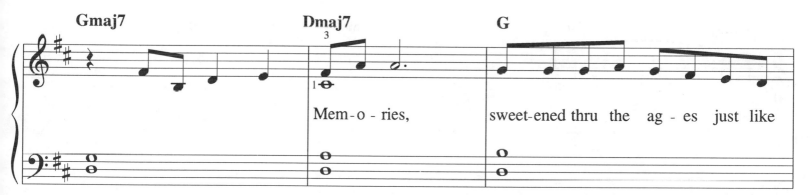

Mem - o - ries, sweet-ened thru the ag - es just like

wine. Qui - et thoughts come float - ing down and

68

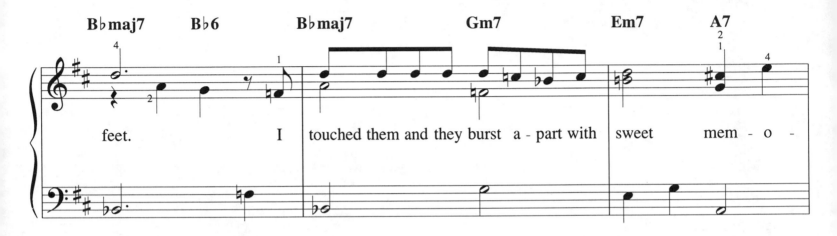

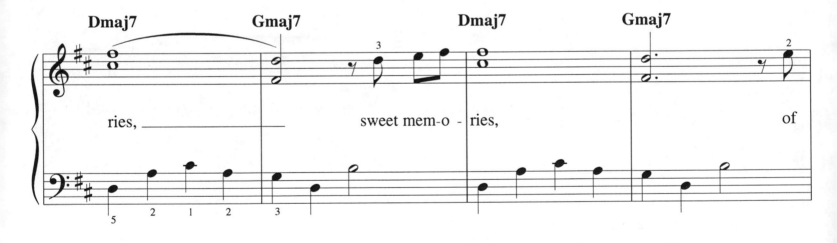

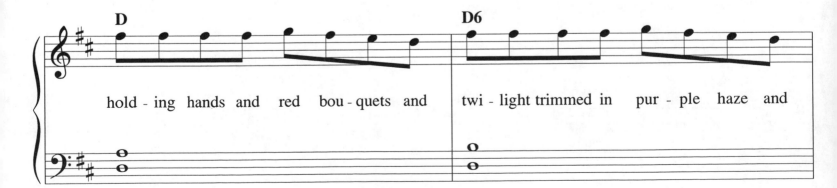

laugh - ing eyes and sim - ple ways and qui - et nights and gen - tle days with

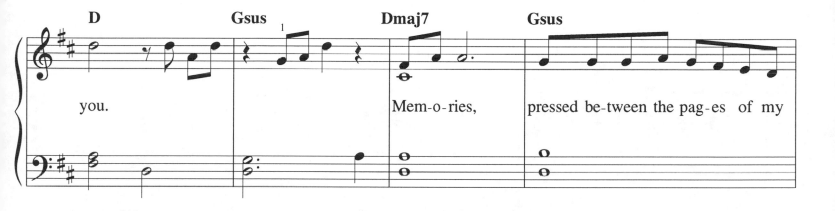

you. Mem-o-ries, pressed be-tween the pag-es of my

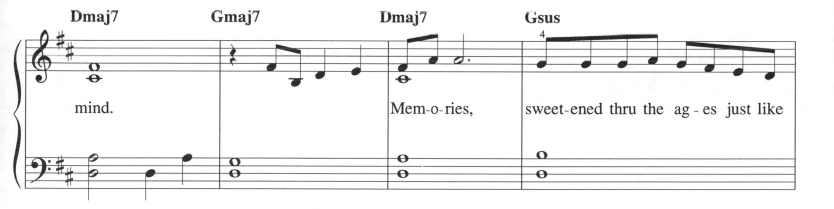

mind. Mem-o-ries, sweet-ened thru the ag-es just like

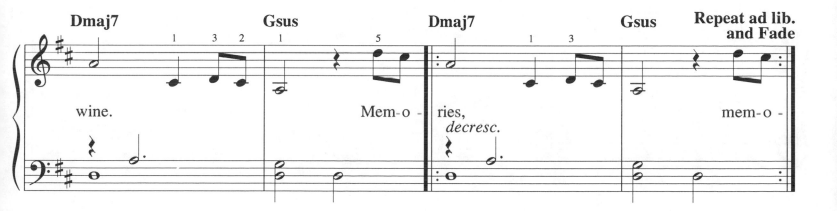

wine. Mem-o - ries, mem-o -

MAKE THE WORLD GO AWAY

Words and Music by
HANK COCHRAN

Moderately Slow

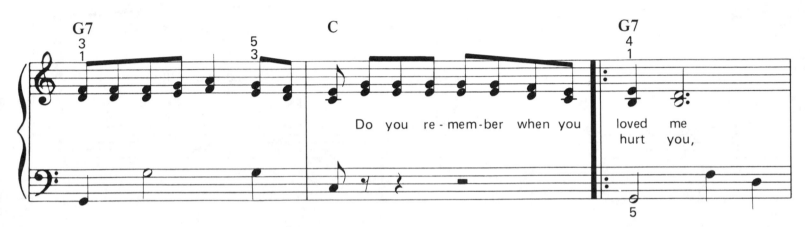

Do you re-mem-ber when you loved me hurt you,

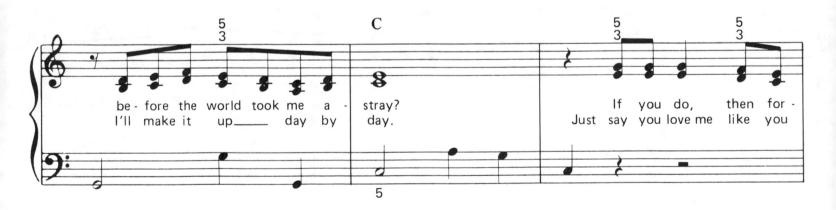

be-fore the world took me a - stray?
I'll make it up___ day by day.

If you do, then for-
Just say you love me like you

give me
used to

and make the world___ go a - way.
and make the world___ go a - way.

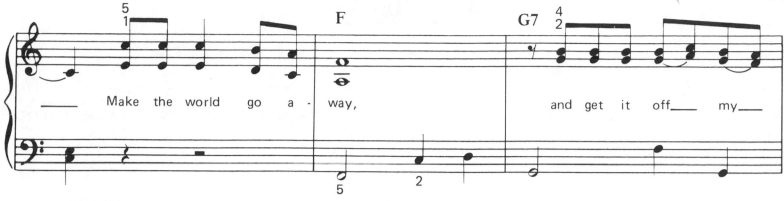

Make the world go a - way, and get it off___ my___

shoul - ders, say the things you used to say,

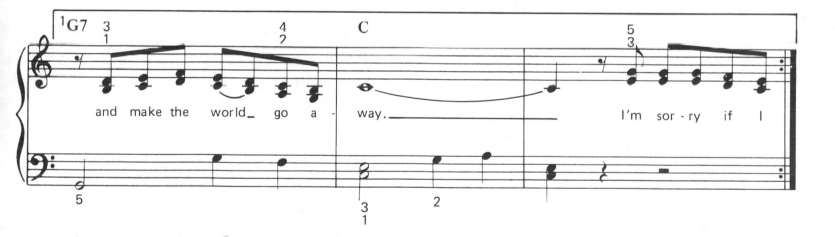

and make the world_ go a - way.___ I'm sor - ry if I

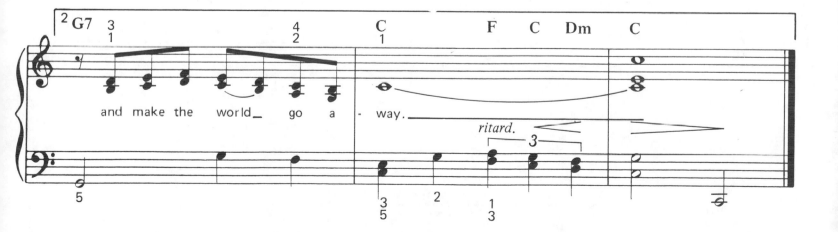

and make the world_ go a - way.___

MY WAY

English Words by PAUL ANKA
Original French Words by GILLES THIBAULT
Music by JACQUES REVAUX and CLAUDE FRANCOIS

Moderately slow

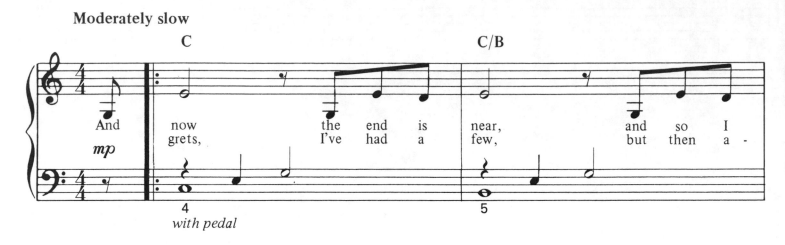

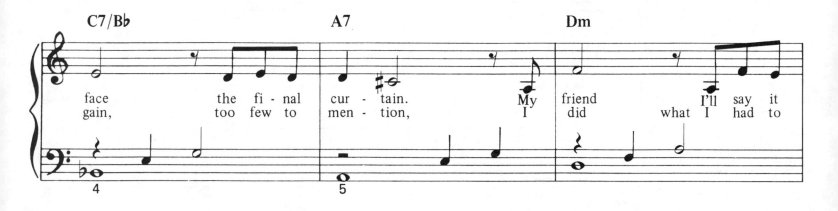

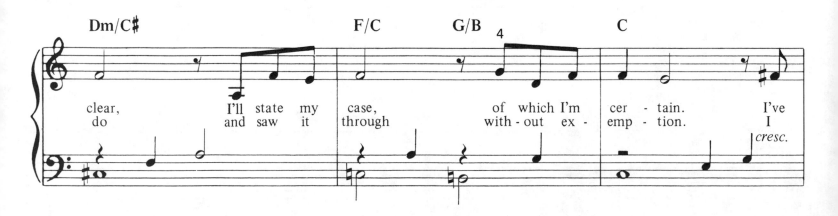

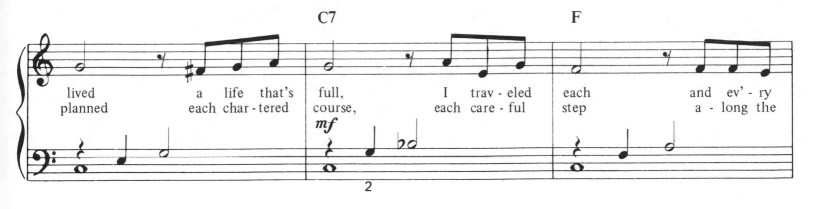

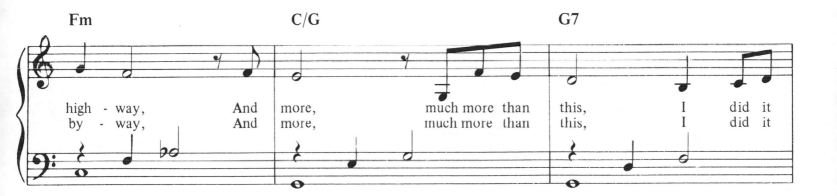

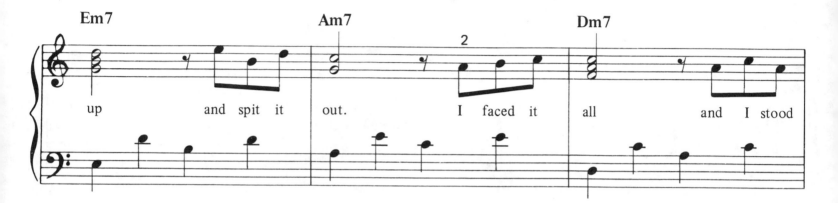

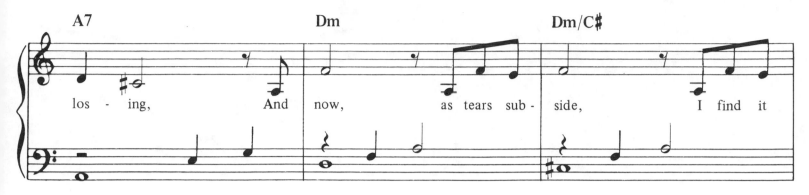

A7 — los - ing, And now, **Dm** as tears sub - **Dm/C#** side, I find it

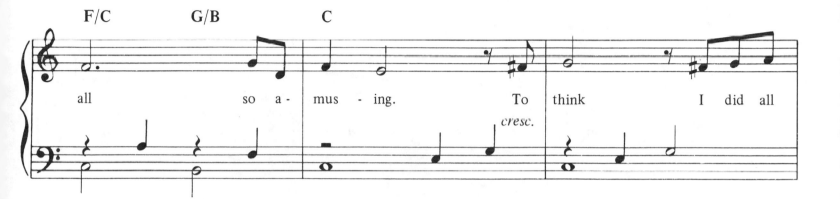

F/C all **G/B** so a - mus - **C** ing. To think I did all

C7 that and may I **F** say, not in a **Fm** shy way, Oh,

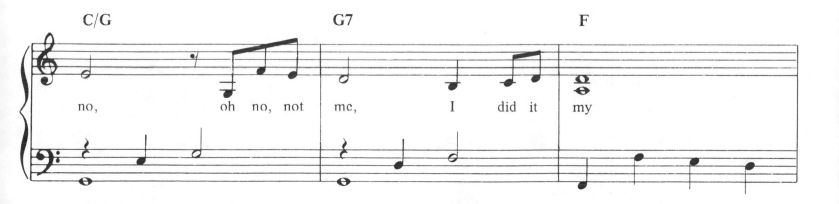

C/G no, oh no, not **G7** me, I did it **F** my

way. For what is a man, what has he got, if not him-

self, then he has not to say the things he tru - ly
cresc. poco a poco

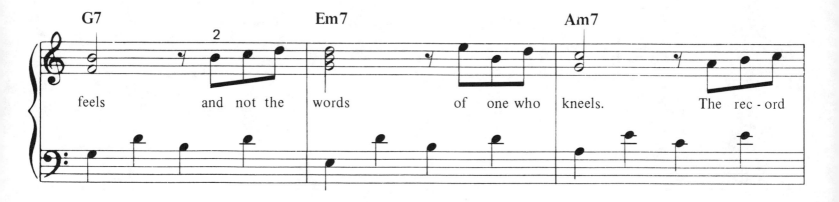

feels and not the words of one who kneels. The rec - ord

shows I took the blows and did it my way.

WEAR MY RING AROUND YOUR NECK

Words and Music by BERT CARROLL
and RUSSELL MOODY

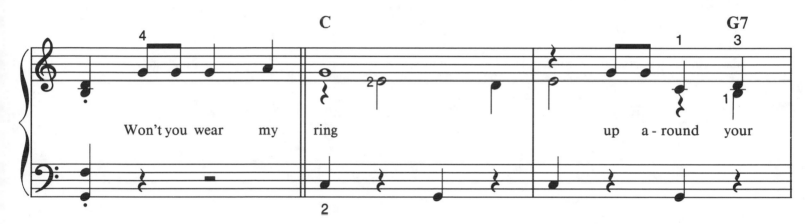

me, _____ And let them see by the

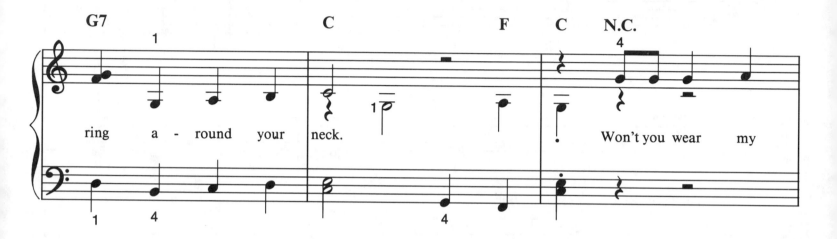

ring a - round your neck. Won't you wear my

ring up a - round your neck

To tell the world I'm yours, by heck.

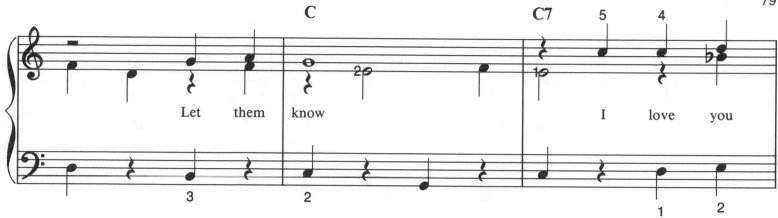

Let them know

I love you

so, And let them know by the

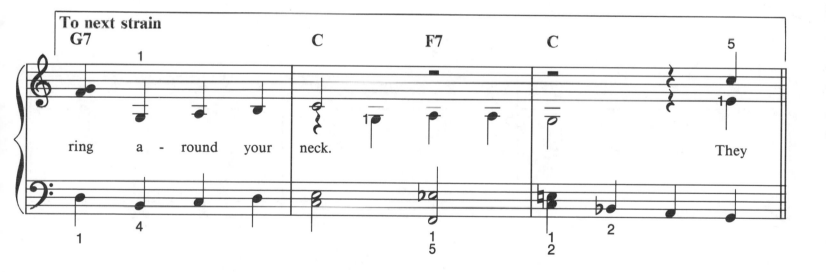

To next strain

ring a - round your neck. They

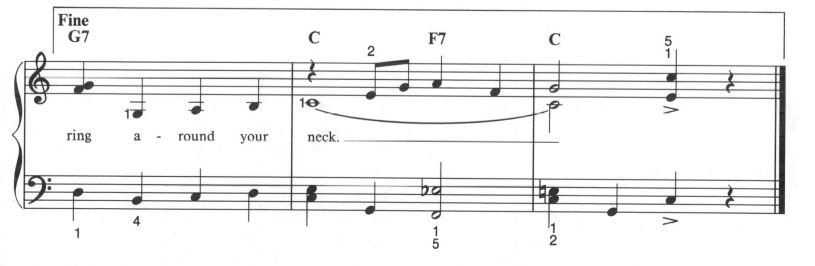

Fine

ring a - round your neck.

say that go - ing stead - y is not the prop - er

thing. They say that we're too young to know the

mean - ing of a ring. I on - ly know I

love_____ you and that you love me too. So,

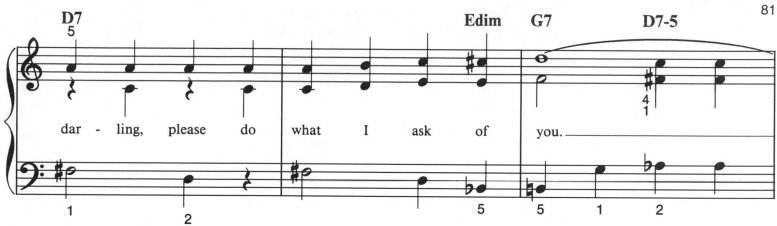

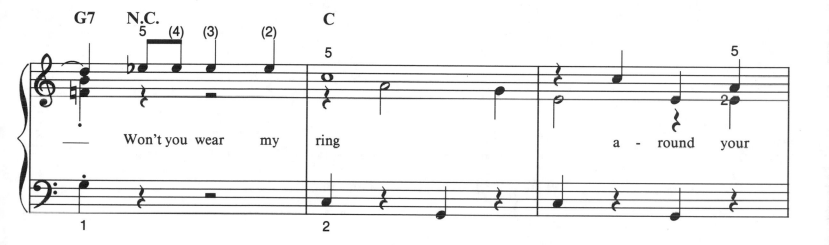

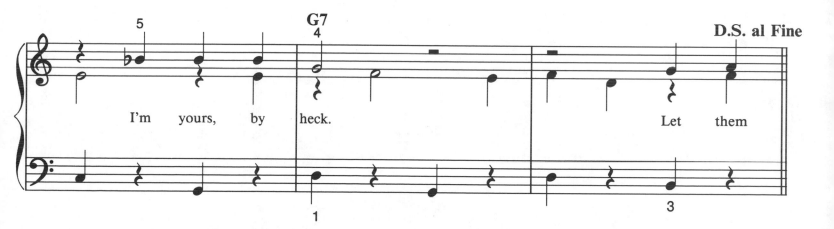

TREAT ME NICE

Words and Music by JERRY LEIBER
and MIKE STOLLER

ev – er kiss me once, ___ kiss me twice. ___
don't want me to be ___ cold as ice, ___

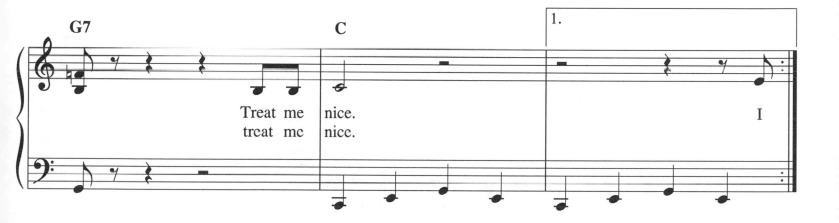

Treat me nice.
treat me nice.

1.

I

2.

Make me feel at home ___

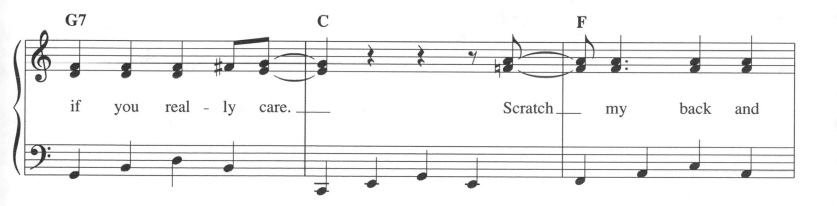

if you real – ly care. ___ Scratch ___ my back and

84

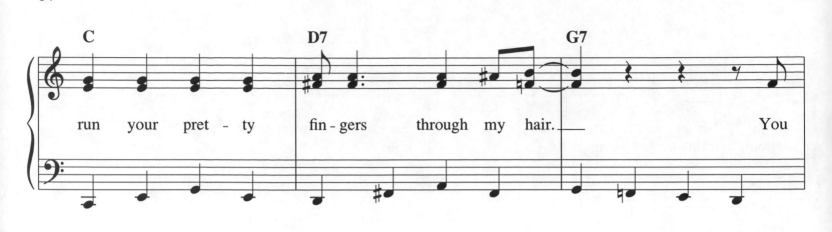

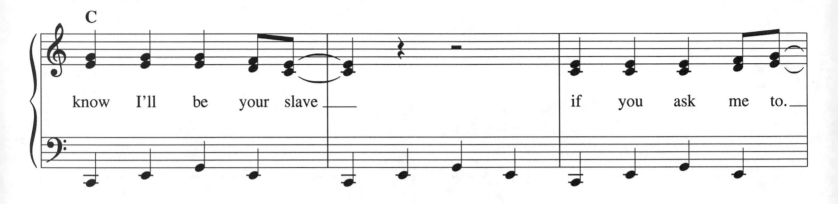

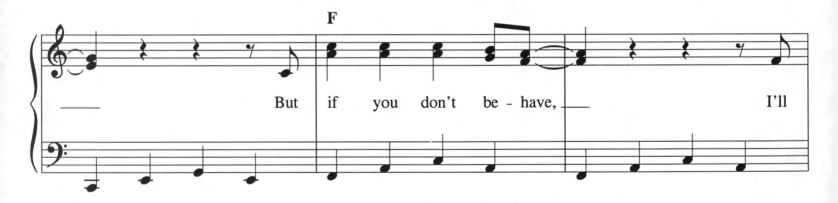

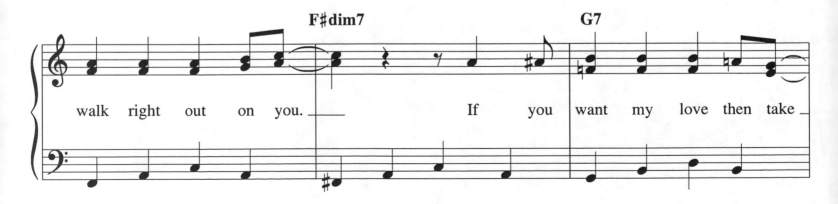

my ad - vice. Treat me

nice. Treat me nice.

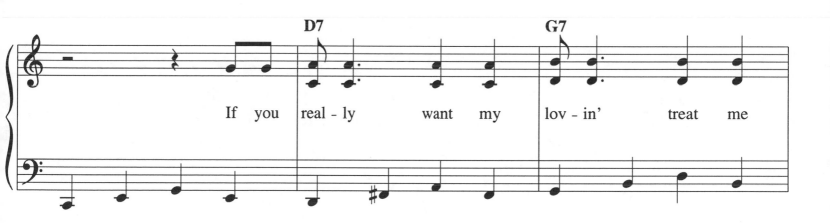

If you real - ly want my lov - in' treat me

nice.

WOODEN HEART

Words and Music by BEN WEISMAN, KAY TWOMEY,
FRED WISE and BERTHOLD KAEMPFERT

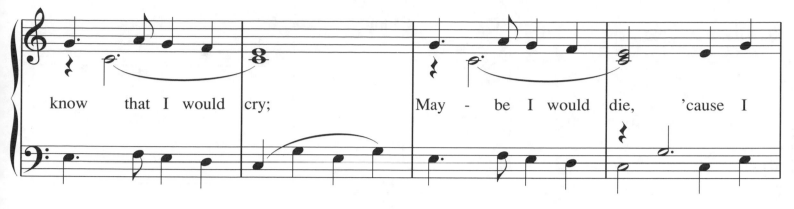

know that I would cry; May - be I would die, 'cause I

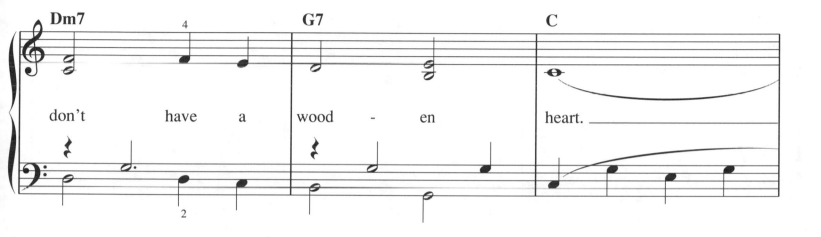

don't have a wood - en heart. _____

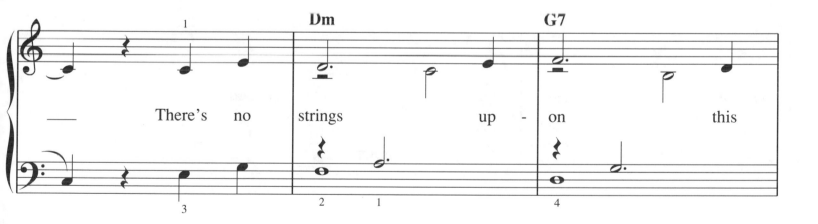

_____ There's no strings up - on this

love of mine; It was al - ways

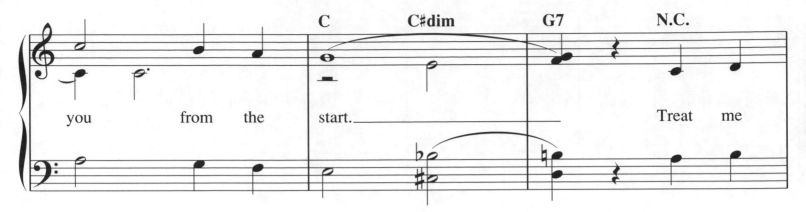

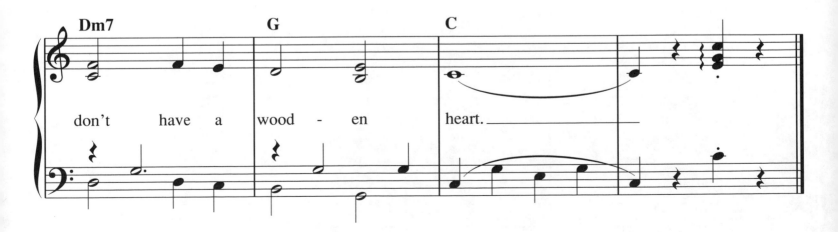